T0021531

For Elizabeth,
best friend, chief merrymaker,
and lover of all things Filipino.

Filipino Celebrations

A Treasury of Feasts and Festivals

text by
Liana Romulo

illustrations by
Corazon Dandan-Albano

TUTTLE Publishing

Tokyo | Rutland, Vermont | Singapore

Welcome to the Philippines!
Mabuhay!

Anyone who knows something about the Philippines can tell you that Filipinos love a good party, and that we celebrate many different kinds of occasions—harvest time, a baby's first birthday, the incoming new year, historical events, and so on. Even the most solemn Roman Catholic holidays, like All Souls' Day, are more like celebrations than formal rituals.

Christmas star lantern

parol

foreign influences

A lot of foreign influences impact our celebrations: We adopted many of Spain's traditions and practices; most significant of all, Christianity. We follow some American practices, too, as well as many Chinese traditions. Perhaps our most cherished holiday of all is Christmas. A great many Filipinos, no matter where they live in the world, come home to be with their families for the season.

sweet fried noodles

tinagtag

other important celebrations

Most other Philippine celebrations are also Christian, including Easter and *barrio* festivals honoring saints. Although *barrio fiestas* are further evidence of Spain's influence, these gatherings also showcase—at its best—Filipino hospitality and community spirit. At *fiesta* time, guests (even tourists) are welcome to wander into any house in the *barrio*, where the hosts will feed and entertain them.

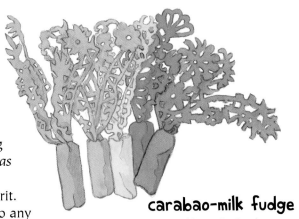

carabao-milk fudge

pastillas de leche

sticky rice wrapped in palm leaves
suman

sticky rice cake
tikoy

a parade
parada

historical influences

Before the Spanish came, Arab missionaries had already introduced Islam to certain parts of the country, and a few hundred Chinese merchants and traders lived on the Islands. Today, some Filipinos (mostly in the south) observe Muslim festivals, such as the Prophet Mohammed's birth celebration.

Since early times, indigenous tribal Filipinos celebrated special occasions, like a baby's birth or getting married. A shaman presided over the preparation of the thanksgiving gifts to be offered to the gods. Old tribal customs continued even after the Spanish arrived, but Catholic saints replaced native gods. If you wanted to become pregnant, for example, you prayed to Santa Clara instead of the native god of fertility. For healing the sick, Filipinos prayed to San Roque; and the rice god Lacanbaco became San Isidro Labrador.

When the Americans came to rule in 1901, they introduced their own festivals and celebrations. The Americans brought us beauty contests, like the Manila Carnival; they also taught us to sing the Happy Birthday Song and helped us create non-religious holidays, like Independence Day and Rizal Day.

There are a great variety of festivals in the Philippines, therefore—a mix of local and foreign flavors, sights, and sounds. Though it can be hard to understand the complex layers of some celebrations, and even a local might not be able to explain it to you, any occasion you go to will almost certainly involve music, laughter, games, and a whole lot of feasting.

fruit cake
cake flavored with liquor

Birthdays
Mga Kaarawan

Cakes and birthday parties came to the Philippines during the American occupation, as did party hats, confetti, and the practice of singing the Happy Birthday Song. The Filipino way of celebrating birthdays in the old days was quite different. Family and friends prepared to greet the birthday celebrant very early in the morning, before he or she woke up, in a practice called the *mañanita*. They would sing and bring food to the birthday celebrant.

Why is pansit served at birthday parties?

Pansit represents long life. Just like in Chinese culture, serving noodles at birthday celebrations ensures a long, healthy life for the celebrant.

first birthday, first haircut
A child's first birthday is considered a big deal, and is celebrated with a party . . . and a first haircut. In some regions the baby's parents ask their smartest relative to perform the ritual cutting, so that the baby will love school when he or she grows up.

scissors
gunting

dog
aso

milk
gatas

Happy Birthday Song
Maligayang bati

Maligayang bati
sa iyong pagsilang.
Maligayang maligayang
maligayang bati!

a hat
sumbrero

balloons
mga lobo

candles
mga kandila

a present
regalo

ISABEL and PAOLO

turning seven
A child's seventh birthday
is also an important mile-
stone, as it marks the start
of middle childhood.

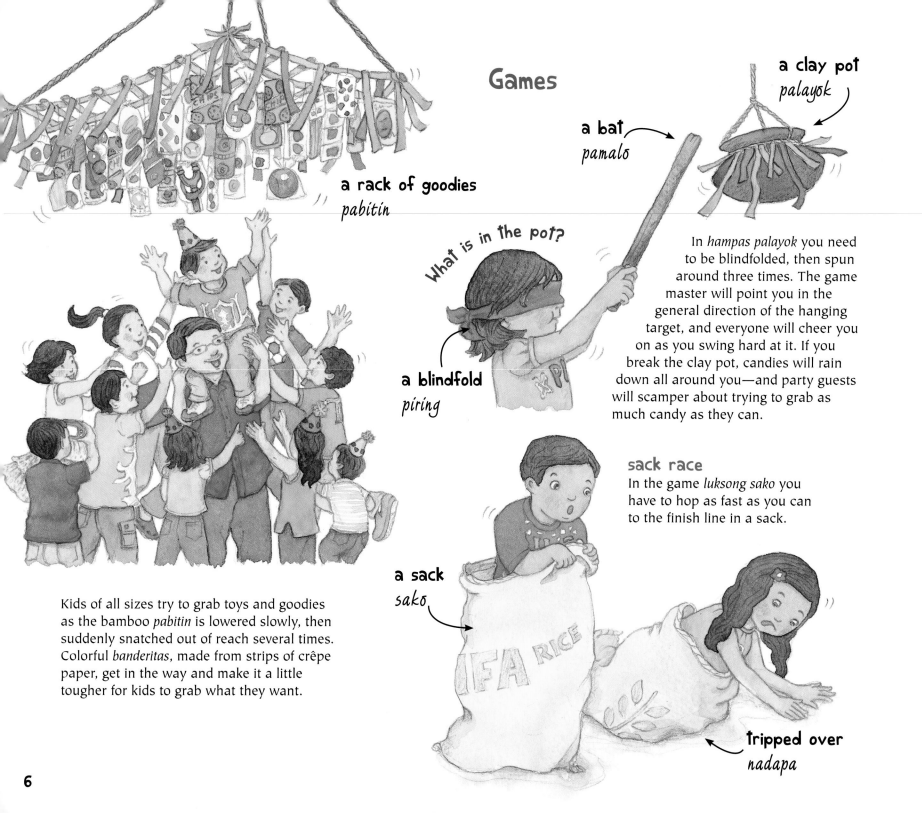

Games

a rack of goodies
pabitin

a bat
pamalo

a clay pot
palayok

What is in the pot?

a blindfold
piring

In *hampas palayok* you need to be blindfolded, then spun around three times. The game master will point you in the general direction of the hanging target, and everyone will cheer you on as you swing hard at it. If you break the clay pot, candies will rain down all around you—and party guests will scamper about trying to grab as much candy as they can.

sack race
In the game *luksong sako* you have to hop as fast as you can to the finish line in a sack.

a sack
sako

IFA RICE

Kids of all sizes try to grab toys and goodies as the bamboo *pabitin* is lowered slowly, then suddenly snatched out of reach several times. Colorful *banderitas*, made from strips of crêpe paper, get in the way and make it a little tougher for kids to grab what they want.

tripped over
nadapa

A Debut

When a girl turns eighteen her parents get ready to present her to society with a social dance called a debut. Just like in other cultures that practice this tradition, the debutant usually wears a formal gown to the grand party, which is often held at a hotel or banquet hall. The first dance of the evening is always performed by the celebrant and her father.

What is a cotillón?

debutant
debutante

father
ama

guests
mga bisita

friends
mga kaibigan

Our former motherland, Spain, introduced us to the debut tradition, so *cotillón* is a Spanish word. Eighteen of the debutant's closest male friends dance in her *cotillón*, an elegant rehearsed ballroom dance, along with eighteen of her best female friends.

Women and girls most dear to the celebrant then light eighteen candles, one at a time, to symbolize the "light" or guidance they will offer her as she makes her transition into womanhood. Very often the debutant's mother lights the final candle and says a few words.

Each of the boys presents the debutant with a single rose, usually before the dance.

Holy Week
Semana Santa

ash
abo

palm leaf
palaspas

All over the world *Semana Santa*, or Holy Week, is the most important week of the Christian calendar. It includes several religious holidays—Palm Sunday, Holy Thursday, and Good Friday—and ends the day before Easter Sunday. *Semana Santa* is also the last week of Lent, the forty-day period devoted to honoring the sufferings, death, and resurrection of Jesus Christ. Because the Philippines is mostly Roman Catholic, with parishes on more than seven thousand islands, there are many ways to celebrate *Semana Santa*.

What is the Pasyon?

The *Pasyon* is the story of Jesus Christ's life, death, and resurrection. The first written version dates back to 1704; however, chanting the *Pasyon* began earlier as an oral tradition taught by Spanish missionaries and adapted into native dialect. It is chanted throughout Holy Week.

apostle
apóstol

the foot-washing ritual
ang paghuhugas ng paa

In most churches on Holy Thursday, a priest performs a foot-washing ritual on twelve parishioners. Often they are costumed as apostles.

singing and chanting
pabasa

Pabasa involves singing or chanting the *Pasyon*. In rural villages, both young and old gather together to chant in the streets every day from six in the morning till ten at night, though one can also chant alone, or in pairs, for a couple of hours or for as long as several days in a row.

foot
paa

reading
nagbabasa

8

procession
prusisyon

Stations of the Cross

During *Semana Santa*, we observe the tradition of walking through the Stations of the Cross—key episodes that took place as Christ carried a giant cross on His way to being crucified. Called *Via Crucis*, each station is portrayed through paintings or sculptures displayed in church. For example, in one picture Christ is crowned with thorns; in another He is shown falling down. Sometimes a priest leads a procession of life-size statues of the Biblical characters through *barrio* streets as townsfolk watch solemnly from the sidelines, the most traditional and religious among them chanting verses about the life and sufferings of Jesus Christ.

The Seven Last Statements

On Good Friday Catholics relive Christ's last hours on the cross by recalling His seven last statements or *siete palabras*. Mainly we quietly pray, do readings, and reflect; but in some areas of the Philippines churchgoers even act out Christ's suffering before His death. The final words before He died are spoken at precisely 3:00 in the afternoon, the hour of His death: "Father, into your hands I commend my spirit."

cross
krus

Easter Encounter

The *salubong*, which means meeting, takes place early Easter Sunday. This is a typical Easter day scene wherein the grieving Mother of Christ meets her risen Son after His crucifixion. Statues of the Blessed Virgin (wearing a black veil to signify her mourning) and the Risen Christ are carried in procession in opposite directions, to meet later at the plaza or wherever the *salubong* will be held.

In San Fernando, Pampanga, and also in a few other towns across the archipelago, Christ's crucifixion is re-enacted, with volunteers happy to have themselves actually nailed to a cross.

a soldier
sundalo

a cape
kapa

a spear
sibat

The Moriones Festival

On the island of Marinduque the colorful Moriones Festival takes place throughout the Holy Week. Devotees put on painted masks and headdresses, pretending to be Roman soldiers—the frightening men who tormented Christ, whipping and spitting on Him as He struggled under the deadweight of His cross. The Moriones, so-called because of the type of face armor they wore, attend evening processions in various towns, sometimes staging the story of Longinus.

Who is Longinus?

Longinus was a Roman soldier who speared Christ's body after the Crucifixion. A drop of Christ's blood landed in his eye, famously curing his blindness. After this miracle, he converted to Christianity, which is why his fellow soldiers wanted to kill him.

11

Town Festivals
Mga Barrio Fiesta

Each Christian town in the Philippines has a patron saint, and each saint has a feast or *fiesta*. In a typical Filipino *barrio*, *fiesta* is the time of year when everyone comes alive with excitement. Santa Clara, for example, is the patron saint of the northern town of Obando. Every May, the people of Obando look forward to celebrating Santa Clara's day with as many activities as possible, including games and contests, prayers, concerts, art exhibits, food fests, pageants, and so on. Celebrations begin with nine days of morning prayers in church, and the *fiesta* normally lasts three days. Many of those who live away travel home to join in on the fun.

Why do most towns in the Philippines have a patron saint?

During the early period of Spanish colonization, Spanish priests would use *fiesta* to lure farmers into the village to Christianize them. Before long, the local government would spend lavishly for *fiestas*, consuming rice stocks meant for times of famine or hardship. Thus, in 1677, King Charles II of Spain ordered that each town honor not more than one patron saint. Today, patron-saint festivals, or *fiestas patronales*, take place not just in the Philippines but in every town in Spain and other Spanish-speaking nations.

a float
karo

band
banda

12

Panagbenga Festival

Carabao Festival

Higantes Festival

Pahiyas Festival

Parada ng Lechon

Pintados Festival

Dinagyang Festival

Kinabayo Festival

Lanzones Festival

buntings
banderitas

The Philippines

The Philippines is a nation of more than seven thousand islands. This means a great number of us live by the sea, and that we rely heavily on boats for transportation and on fishing for food. It also means we have developed many spoken languages (called "dialects") within islands or groups of islands, though mainly we speak Tagalog and Visaya.

Because the Philippines sits just above the equator, we have warm tropical weather all year round, with a rainy reason, similar to our neighbors in Thailand, Indonesia, and Malaysia. We also have powerful typhoons, like Taiwan above us, several active volcanoes, and earthquakes that shake us up from time to time.

Though we have a lot in common with our Southeast Asian neighbors, we are also quite different from them because the great majority of us are Catholic and because English is widely spoken throughout the country.

13

Viva Santo Niño!

When the Spanish explorer Ferdinand Magellan arrived in Cebu in 1521, he gave the chieftain's wife a statue of the Infant Jesus, the Santo Niño. It was a gift that symbolized friendship and celebrated the native couple's baptism into Catholicism. Forty-four years later, another explorer—Miguel López de Legazpi—invaded Cebu, burning an entire village to the ground. Miraculously the statue survived, and the Santo Niño was worshipped from then on.

The Santo Niño has a large following of devotees all over the Philippines, most especially in Cebu, Kalibo, and Iloilo—three places that celebrate His feast day in very big ways.

Celebrating Filipino History: The Ati-atihan Festival
Kalibo * 3rd Sunday of January

The Ati-atihan festival celebrates the part of our history when the natives made friends with the Malays who came to the Islands from the south. The highlight is when groups representing different tribes compete in street dancing, wearing tribal costumes and elaborate headdresses.

Cebu's Sinulog Parade Festival
Cebu * 3rd week of January

Weeks of preparation and days of celebration lead up to Cebu's biggest festival. The main event is a parade that snakes around the city, with floats and teams of dancers competing for the Mayor's Prize. Everyone gets dressed up in wild colors and darkens their faces with soot.

What does sinulog mean?

In the local dialect of Cebu, the root word of *sinulog* means current. The *sinulog* dance mimics the ebb and flow of the river.

Dinagyang Street Dancing
Iloilo * 4th week of January

Street dancing and the Miss Dinagyang contest feature prominently in Iloilo's Santo Niño festival. Performers paint their skin brown and wear costumes made from indigenous materials, like shells and feathers.

a drum
tambol

How to make an Ati-atihan mask

To make a mask you'll need a paper plate, pen or pencil, paint, crafts glue, cardboard pieces in different colors, crêpe paper, and various odds and ends to use as embellishments: yarn, beads, sequins, feathers, etc. You will also need a paintbrush, scissors, and a hole puncher.

1 Hold the paper plate up to your face and mark where you want to cut eye holes, then cut them out. Punch 2 small holes at the edge of your mask where your ears will be.

2 Paint the entire plate black. Let it dry. Then paint in the nose, mouth, and cheeks.

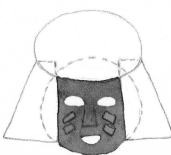

3 Cut different shapes of cardboard and paste them on your mask.

4 Embellish your mask with crêpe paper, sequins, beads, and whatever you can find.

5 Attach feathers to the top edge of your mask. Cut 2 pieces of yarn and tie them into the ear holes. Use the yarn to tie the mask onto your face.

Local Harvest Festivals

Both the Pahiyas and the Carabao Festivals honor San Isidro Labrador. These take place in May, at the peak of when most harvests occur. Like Thanksgiving in Canada, the United States, or Great Britain, these festivals give thanks to God for abundant food and good crops.

The San Isidro Labrador Harvest Festival

As the patron saint of farmers, several farming towns pay homage to him, including Lucban (Quezon), Pulilan (Bulacan), Agdangan (Quezon), Nabas (Aklan), and Talavera (Nueva Ecija).

house
bahay

rice wafer
kiping

The Pahiyas Thanksgiving Festival
Lucban, Quezon * 15th of May

The Pahiyas Festival (in the town of Lucban) is a big colorful celebration. Before Spanish times, it was just a simple thanksgiving celebration offered to the *anitos* (spirits). After the Spaniards arrived, bringing with them Catholicism, farmers started to bring their best harvests to the church for blessing. Later on, with better and more plentiful harvests, they started decorating their houses—both inside and out—with food. The locals string fruits, flowers, and vegetables together, using them to frame windows and doors, and create giant flower blossoms and elaborate chandeliers with *kiping* (rice wafer) of every color.

How to make kiping

1 Select about 100 nicely shaped fresh leaves in similar sizes. These will be used as molds for the *kiping*.

a leaf
dahon

2 You may trim the leaves with scissors to make them more uniform. Wash and dry them thoroughly.

3 Soak 1½ kilos of rice in water. After 2 hours, grind the mixture to form a paste, adding water if necessary. Mix in 12 packets of food coloring and 2½ tablespoons of rock salt.

4 Spread the paste thinly on the fresh leaves and steam for 5 minutes. After steaming, dry the *kiping* in a shaded area.

a wok
kawali

5 Peel off the *kiping* individually and pile them together. Put a wooden chopping board or other heavy object on top of the *kiping* for at least half a day.

6 Separate the *kiping* and let them dry.

The Carabao Festival
Pulilan, Bulacan * 14th of May

Preparations for the Carabao Festival begin early in the morning. The carabaos, or water buffaloes, are shaved clean, and their horns and hooves are rubbed with oil to make them shine. Wearing beautiful garlands, the carabaos parade around town, compete in races, and kneel before the church. Some even walk on their knees to pay respect to San Isidro.

a farmer
magsasaka

a carabao or water buffalo
kalabaw

17

Other Feasts Honoring Saints

The word *fiesta* means feast in Spanish, and *barrio fiestas* (town festivals) celebrate the feast day of a particular town's patron saint. There are more than one thousand five hundred towns in the country, and hundreds of *barrio fiestas*.

a horse
kabayo

The Kinabayo Festival
Dapitan City, Zamboanga del Norte * 25th of July

The Kinabayo Festival, in honor of St. James, recalls the Christians' fierce battles against the Muslims who reigned over Spain. At the center of Kinabayo is a parade in which participants—representing the Christians and the Muslims—portray warring soldiers riding on horses made of rattan and bamboo.

The Lechon of Saint John
Balayan, Batangas * 24th of June

To celebrate the feast of St. John the Baptist, the people of Balayan organize a grand parade of about a hundred succulent roast pigs fully dressed in curly wigs, sunglasses, raincoats, and other garments.

a roasted pig
lechon

a giant
higante

The Higantes Festival
Angono, Rizal
* 23rd of November

This festival honors San Clemente, the patron saint of fishermen. The main procession, which ends at Laguna de Bay, features not only a statue of San Clemente but also *pahadores* (devotees carrying boat paddles, nets, traps, and other fishing gear) and *higantes* (paper-mâché giants measuring more than three meters high).

The Kasilonawan Festival
Obando, Bulacan * 18th of May

An ancient fertility ritual, the Kasilonawan Festival honors Santa Clara, patron saint of the childless. Devotees sing and dance, moving in procession toward the town church. Many visitors travel a great distance to participate in the ceremonies, hoping to conceive a baby.

dance
sayaw

The Feast of the Black Nazarene
Quiapo, Manila * 9th of January

As one of the most popular religious festivals in the Philippines, this feast day honors the dark-skinned statue of Jesus Christ, called the Black Nazarene. Carved in Mexico, the life-size statue arrived onboard a Galleon ship from Mexico in 1606. Millions of Filipinos believe that devotion to the Black Nazarene will bring health, prosperity, protection, and good luck.

a devotee
deboto

The Peñafrancia Madonna Festival
Naga City * 3rd Saturday of September

During this feast, which takes place at night on the river, a candlelit procession of boats transports a statue of the Madonna back to its shrine at the Naga Cathedral. The Madonna is believed to have miraculous powers.

Festivals Celebrating Philippine History

Just as Americans commemorate the day Christopher Columbus landed in the New World, Filipinos celebrate various events that helped shaped the nation.

a weapon
sandata

a warrior
mandirigma

a shield
kalasag

The Pintados Festival
Leyte * 29th of June

La Isla de los Pintados (Island of the Painted Ones) is how the Spanish referred to the Philippine Visayan islands when they first landed there. This is because the native warriors wore tribal tattoos, very often covering their entire bodies, as if painted from head to toe. Eventually, Spanish priests banned tattoos because they believed them to be savage and evil. The Pintados Festival showcases the ancient heritage of the people of Leyte and Samar through music, dance, and—of course—body painting.

Sikatuna

Miguel López de Legazpi

The Sandugo Festival
Bohol * 25th of March

There is an ancient ritual in the Philippines called, in Spanish, *pacto de sangre*, where tribal members would cut open a wrist, bleed into a cup filled with liquid, and drink each other's blood. This act symbolized peace and friendship. The most famous example of this practice is Sandugo, which took place in Bohol in 1565 between the Spanish explorer Miguel López de Legazpi and Datu Sikatuna, the chieftain of Bohol. Parades, pageants, street dancing, and fireworks combine to commemorate Sandugo.

Fiestas Just for Fun

Some festivals don't have any historical or religious significance, like the Tuna Festival in General Santos City, a center for seafood. Another is the Bankero Festival, which honors boatmen, in Pagsanjan, Laguna.

The Panagbenga Festival
Baguio City * Month of February

The Panagbenga Festival takes place in the mountain city of Baguio for the whole month of February. Also known as the Baguio Flower Festival, activities include flower exhibits, garden tours, floral contests, a colorful flower parade, and an outdoor flea market.

The Lanzones Festival
Camiguin Island * 3rd week of October

Camiguin Island, along the coast of Mindanao, is known for the sweetness of its lanzones fruit. Every year, at harvest time, locals and tourists enjoy a four-day thanksgiving celebration that includes street dancing, exhibits, beauty pageants, and a grand parade. Houses, streetlamps, and even people are decorated with lanzones fruits.

lanzones

21

Typical Fiesta Activities

Some town festivals are popular, and attended by throngs of curious visitors who look forward to participating in various activities.

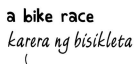
a bike race
karera ng bisikleta

basketball

sports fests
mga palaro ng palakasan

Sports competitions and other games are important in typical *barrio fiestas*. Basketball, which we inherited during the American period, is perhaps the most popular sport in the country, but cockfighting remains a sporting activity in many festivals.

pole-climbing
palosebo

In the game called *palosebo*, kids and grownups take turns climbing a greased bamboo pole with prize money on top. Whoever can climb the pole to the top gets to keep the money.

beauty pageants
patimpalak ng kagandahan

Lovely young ladies join beauty contests, their escorts squirming next to them in starched barongs and stiff new shoes.

singing contests
patimpalak ng kantahan

Filipinos love singing, dancing, and performing in general—and *fiesta* is the perfect outlet for showcasing people's talents. Oratorical contests are sometimes part of the program, too, though they are not as popular as they used to be.

The Town Fair

Town fairs (*mga perya*) are often around during *barrio fiestas*, adding immensely to the festive feeling. At night the *perya* comes alive as people (still referred to as *feriantes*, which is a Spanish word) enjoy the rides and mill about, stopping from stall to stall.

a fortune teller
manghuhula

rides
mga sakayan

beto-beto
In this game of luck, the "banker" shakes three dice inside a bowl-like receptacle covered with a plate while gamblers place bets on numbers on a board.

fairs showcasing local products
Some fairs are focused on selling local handicrafts and products, like sweets made from mangoes, *ube* (purple yam), tamarind, and carabao's milk.

handicrafts
sining ng mga gawaing-kamay

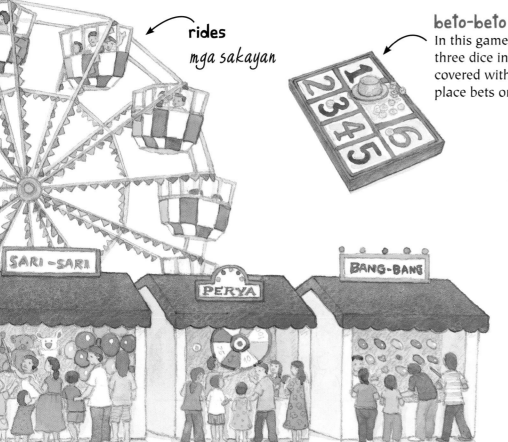

seashells
mga kabibe

sweets
minatamis

games
mga palaro

Bingo, shooting targets, and darts are some typical games.

stalls
mga tindahan

Some stalls feature games with prizes; others offer popcorn, cotton candy, and other types of refreshments.

The Flowers of May Celebrations
Flores de Mayo

In the Flores de Mayo, which takes place all over the country for the whole month of May, little girls and young ladies in beautiful gowns offer flowers to the Virgin Mary. The highlight of the celebration is the Santa Cruzan, the procession in honor of Reyna Elena, who searched for the cross upon which Jesus Christ was crucified. It is a great honor to be selected to play either the role of Reyna Elena, the Queen Elena, or any one of the other queens—the Reyna de las Flores (Queen of Flowers), the Reyna Fe (Queen of Faith), or the Reyna de las Virgenes (Queen of Virgins).

The Virgin Mary
ang Mahal na Birhen

princess
sagala

Reyna ELENA

de las FLORES

Reyna de las VIRGENES

queen
reyna

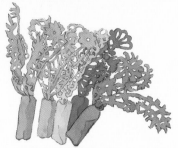

carabao-milk fudge
pastillas de Leche

How to make pastillas de leche

In earlier times, *pastillas*—beautifully wrapped in colored paper—were served only at *fiesta* time. Dry and crisp on the outside, and soft and moist on the inside, *pastillas* still make great party treats. Carabao's milk is fatty and rich in taste; but since it is not readily available all over the world, here's how to make *pastillas* using cow's milk:

You'll need

| 1¼ cups (300 ml) sweetened condensed milk | 2 cups (450 grams) sifted powdered milk | ¼ tsp grated lemon rind | ½ cup confectioner's sugar, for rolling | Wax paper and colored tissue paper for wrapping |

1 Combine condensed milk, powdered milk, and lemon rind.

2 Mix and blend the ingredients evenly.

3 Dust a large cutting board with confectioner's sugar.

4 Flatten the mixture on the cutting board with a rolling pin until it is ½ inch (12 mm) thick.

5 Cut it into 2 x 1 inch (5 X 2.5 cm) lengths.

6 Cut the wax paper into 2 x 5 inch (5 x 12 cm) strips and wrap each piece in wax paper. Then wrap it in tissue paper of different colors.

a spoon and a fork
kutsara at tinidor

Baptisms
Mga Binyag

gifts
mga regalo

Godparents are expected to bring gifts of value to the baptism, like jewelry, a sterling-silver spoon-and-fork set, or a stroller.

Baptism is the first religious ritual in any child's life, and it is the most important. The parents name their baby during baptism, and also assign at least one godfather and one godmother to look after him or her. At Christmas and on the child's birthday, godparents are supposed to give the child the best gifts. A priest performs the baptismal ceremony, pouring water on the baby's forehead to symbolize that the baby has joined the Church.

earrings
mga hikaw

a shower of coins
paghagis ng mga barya

Traditionally godparents shower coins at the after-party, to make sure the baby will have a lot of money in her life. Children squeal in delight as they scramble around, filling their pockets with coins.

gift money
pakimkim

It is also common for godparents to give money as a present, called *pakimkim*.

Why do babies wear white gowns at their baptism?

White symbolizes the purity God gives to newborn babies. Often families use a gown that has been passed down from one generation to the next.

godfather
ninong

godmother
ninang

parents
mga magulang

priest
pari

godchild
inaanak

cousin
pinsan

siblings
mga kapatid

a monument
monumento

the flag
ang watawat

Independence Day
Araw ng Kalayaan

After gaining independence in 1946, we began celebrating June 12, when Philippine independence from Spain was proclaimed, and December 30, when our national hero, Jose Rizal, was executed by the Spanish in 1896. On June 12, cars fly miniature flags, and streets throughout the country come alive with the Philippine colors. The President leads a parade in Manila, while smaller parades take place in towns and cities everywhere, even in New York and Rome, where there are large Filipino communities.

Jose Rizal
Flag-raising and wreath-laying ceremonies take place at Luneta Park, Manila, on December 30, in honor of Jose Rizal, who died near the spot where his monument is today.

Emilio Aguinaldo
On June 12, 1898, Philippine independence from Spain was proclaimed at the home of Emilio Aguinaldo, our first president, in the town of Kawit, in the province of Cavite.

people
mga tao

The Philippine Flag

A group of Filipino rebels signed a truce with Spain in 1897, which required them to leave the Philippines and live overseas. They created the national flag in Hong Kong, returned to their homeland, and flew the flag in battle on May 28, 1898. During the proclamation of Philippine independence two weeks later in Kawit, Cavite, the flag was formally raised, blue above red.

Can you guess why this flag is upside-down?

In 1899 war broke out between the Philippines and the United States. The flag was flown with the red field up to show that a state of hostility existed.

The three stars signified the three principal islands of the Philippine archipelago: Luzon, the Visayas, and Mindanao.

The eight rays of the sun signified the eight provinces that revolted and were put under martial law by the Spaniards during the start of the Philippine Revolution in 1896: Manila, Cavite, Bulacan, Pampanga, Nueva Ecija, Bataan, Laguna, and Batangas.

The colors blue, red, and white mirrored those of the United States flag, and were intended to express gratitude toward Americans for helping us regain our independence from Spain. Little did we know that the United States would immediately take over as our colonizers, and make it illegal to display the flag from 1902 to 1919.

The white triangle represented the Katipunan, the secret revolutionary society, of which the flag's creators were members.

Who made the first Philippine flag?

Marcela Marino de Agoncillo sewed the first flag with the help of her eldest daughter, Lorenza, and Delfina Herbosa de Natividad.

29

All Souls' Day
Araw ng mga Patay

a picture
larawan

food
pagkain

Filipinos start preparing for *Araw ng mga Patay* long before the actual day, which falls on November 2. We flock to cemeteries, where leaves need to be raked, flowers planted, and gravestones cleaned. To give respect to our ancestors, which is what this holiday is for, their burial plots need to be tidy. We usually spend the day at the cemetery with our families. We bring picnic baskets filled with food, we sit around and chat, and sometimes we pray. Many hold all-night vigils and light candles over tombstones. A priest might even give a brief ceremony, but for most of the day the mood is easygoing and relaxed, with refreshments flowing freely and perhaps even a *mahjong* table set up next to the grave.

a statue
rebulto

songs of prayers for the departed
pangangaluluwa

On the eve of All Souls' Day people go from house to house singing songs dedicated to the departed souls who may still be circulating in the neighborhood searching for prayers. After the *pangangaluluwa* your neighbors might offer you money, ginger tea, and something to eat.

a guitar
gitara

candle drippings
mga tulo ng kandila

Kids have fun collecting candle drippings and shaping them into balls and other shapes.

a tomb
nitso

30

praying the rosary
nagrorosaryo

a rosary
rosaryo

widow
byuda

a child
bata

cemetery
sementeryo

candles and food for the dead
mga kandila at pagkain para sa mga patay

It is common for people to light candles and put out small plates of food for the dead to "eat." Pictures of loved ones who have died might also be displayed at the burial site.

newlyweds
bagong kasal

Weddings
Mga Kasal

Filipino weddings are grand affairs, with cousins, aunts, uncles, nieces, nephews, and relatives—even little babies—*all* present, as well as a good many other guests. With the bride gowned in white and a bouquet toss at the reception, western influence is strong, but a good many local superstitions are strictly minded, too. Not only that: traditional church rituals are almost always performed.

Men and women whom the bride and groom know well and respect, perhaps aunts and uncles, play important roles in the ceremony as *ninongs* and *ninangs*. They are, essentially, godparents (also referred to as "principal sponsors") who can attest that the couple is ready for marriage.

Close friends of the couple, around their age, also form part of the entourage as "secondary sponsors." They are in charge of bearing wedding coins, lighting the candles, and handling the veil and cord.

the money dance
ang sayaw ng pera

In a practice that is common among northern Filipinos, wedding guests pin money onto the bride's gown and the groom's *barong* while the couple dances. The newlyweds then keep the cash to spend as they wish.

flowers
mga bulaklak

maid of honor
binibining pandangal

Bible
Bibliya

best man
piling ginoo

bridesmaids
mga abay

groom
lalaki

groomsmen
mga abay

ring bearer
tagapaghatid ng singsing

bride
babae

flower girls
mga tagapag-alay ng bulaklak

female principal sponsor
ninang

male principal sponsor
ninong

Wedding Symbols

veil
belo

The veil that goes over the groom's shoulders and the bride's head is a prayer for protection during marriage.

candles
mga kandila

The ceremony of lighting the candles is a call for enlightenment, and also a reminder of God's presence in the ceremony.

unity cord
yugal

A cord will join loosely the necks of both bride and groom, in the form of a number eight. This symbolizes a union that lasts forever.

wedding rings
mga singsing

As it is all over the world, the wedding ring—whose shape has no beginning and no end—signifies unending, eternal love.

Superstitions

Every good Filipina knows that she mustn't try on her wedding dress just before the big day. If she does, the wedding might not push through.

coins
arras

Thirteen pieces of either gold or silver coins signify the groom's promise to take care of his wife and children.

Why is a chamber pot considered a suitable wedding gift?

chamber pot
arinola

An *arinola* brings good luck to newlyweds.

prohibitions
sukob sa taon

Two siblings must not marry in the same year. That's called *sukob sa taon*, and it's bad luck!

2013 DEC 31 Ate's Wedding Day!

2014 JAN 1 Kuya's Wedding Day!

Meeting of the Families

After the couple has decided to marry, the *pamanhikan* comes next. That's when the groom—with his parents—visits the bride's family to ask for her hand in marriage. Afterward, the couple will usually make a round of visits to older relatives and friends who were not present during the *pamanhikan*. This gesture of respect is known as *pa-alam*, which literally means "act of letting something be known."

customary gift
The best home-cooked specialty made by the groom's mother makes a perfect gift for the hosts during the *pamanhikan*.

Why do couples offer eggs to Santa Clara?

Couples typically offer eggs to the monastery of Santa Clara before their wedding day, and ask the nuns to pray for a rain-free celebration.

Merry Christmas!
Maligayang Pasko!

Children all over the world love Christmas. Why? Because of the presents, of course! Filipinos look forward to gifts, too, but in the Philippines even the smallest kids know that Christmas is—first of all—baby Jesus's birthday. The Three Wise Men brought gifts to Jesus, and this is why we give each other gifts at Christmastime.

What about Santa Claus and all his reindeer? Well, he didn't come to the Philippines until the Americans came at the beginning of the 20th century, when Spain ended their rule in the country. Today Santa is a big deal at Christmas, along with Christmas trees. If there's one thing that symbolizes a Filipino Christmas, though, it's the *parol*. This five-pointed star lantern represents the bright star of Bethlehem, which guided the Three Wise Men to Jesus.

the star of Bethlehem
parol

Most *parols* today are lit up with flashing electric lights, and are made from plastic and all sorts of materials.

the nativity scene
belen

The *belen*, or scene about the birth of Jesus, is familiar to people in every corner of the Philippines. Simple ones might be found in homes. Elaborate ones, complete with the Three Wise Men and farm animals, decorate churches and office buildings.

string
sinulid

glue
pandikit

How to make a parol

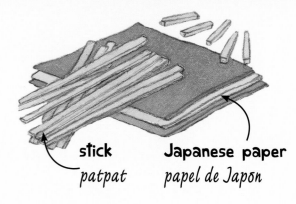

stick
patpat

Japanese paper
papel de Japon

1 Tie 4 sticks together by looping the string around the sticks, a half inch from the ends. Form a "V" by separating the sticks, 2 on each side.

2 Add another 2 sticks to the "V," as shown.

3 Insert 2 more sticks between the others, overlapping them, then make another joint with more string.

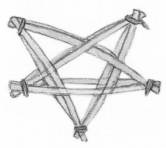

4 Attach the last 2 sticks with string, again in an overlapping pattern.

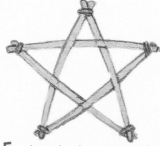

5 Align the frame to make a symmetrical five-sided star.

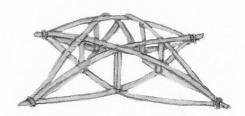

6 Insert the posts at five points by pulling apart the star frame. The tension of the frame will hold the posts in place.

7 Cut triangular pieces of rice paper, apply paste to the frame, and attach the paper. Do the same for the front and back pentagons at the center.

8 Make 2 or 4 tassels, and attach them to the points of the star.

church
simbahan

a bell
kampana

purple-colored rice cake
puto bumbong

purple-colored sweet cooked in bamboo tubes and served in banana leaves

rice cake with cheese and salted egg
bibingka

rice cake baked in special clay pot, topped with cheese and salted egg

ginger
luya

How to make ginger tea (salabat)

1 tbsp fresh ginger root, sliced
2 cups water
honey or brown sugar

1 Boil ginger in water for 5 to 10 minutes.
2 Pour liquid into cups.
3 Add honey or sugar, to taste.

The Nine Masses
Simbang Gabi

Traditionally, the Christmas season begins on December 16, with the first of a series of nine masses called *Simbang Gabi*. Also called *Misas de Gallo*, these thanksgiving masses begin at four o'clock in the morning. A breakfast of *salabat, puto bumbong*, and *bibingka* is offered afterward.

It is hard to get up so early for church—but you can pray for a wish at *Simbang Gabi*, and if you make it to all nine, your wish will come true.

What does gallo mean?

Gallo means rooster in Spanish. Because roosters crow early in the morning, the masses are called *Misas de Gallo*.

a rooster
tandang

Christmas Has Arrived

Ang Pasko ay Sumapit

Christmas songs can be heard everywhere you go. In 1933 Vicente Rubi and
Mariano Vestil composed a song, in the Cebuano dialect, that truly captures the Filipino
Christmas spirit. The famous composer Levi Celerio wrote the Tagalog lyrics later on.

Christmas has arrived	*Ang pasko ay sumapit*
Let us sing	*Tayo ay mangagsiawit*
Beautiful hymns	*Ng magagandang himig*
Because God is love	*Dahil sa ang Diyos ay pag-ibig*
When Christ was born	*Nang si Kristo ay isilang*
There were Three Kings who visited	*May tatlong haring nagsidalaw*
And each one offered	*At ang bawat isa*
Their respective gifts	*Ay nagsipaghandog ng tanging alay*
It's a new year so we must change our lives	*Bagong taon ay magbagong buhay*
So that our people will be glad	*Nang lumigaya ang ating bayan*
Let us strive in order for us to achieve	*Tayo'y magsikap upang makamtan*
Prosperity	*Natin ang kasaganaan*
Let us sing	*Tayo'y mangagsiawit*
While the world is tranquil	*Habang ang mundo'y tahimik*
The day has arrived	*Ang araw ay sumapit*
Of the child that came from heaven	*Ng Sanggol na dulot ng langit*
Let us love one another	*Tayo ay magmahalan*
And follow the golden rule	*Ating sundin ang gintong aral*
And from now on	*At magbuhat ngayon*
Even though it's not Christmas let's share	*Kahit hindi pasko ay magbigayan*

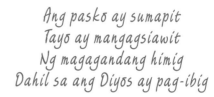

The Holy Family's Journey

Panunuluyan is a pageant about the Holy Family's journey and search for shelter, which usually takes place on Christmas Eve. Kids know by heart how baby Jesus was born in a stable and placed in a manger after Mary and Joseph journeyed from Nazareth to Bethlehem and couldn't find a place to stay.

plant
halaman

hay
dayami

a cow
baka

actors
mga artista

a sheep
tupa

Christmas gift
pamasko

Christmas Eve dinner
Noche Buena

The ninth mass of *Simbang Gabi* takes place on Christmas Eve, or *Noche Buena*, when everyone gets all dressed up and goes to church at midnight. *Noche Buena* means good night in Spanish, but to Filipinos it means eating, drinking, and gift-giving until the wee hours of the morning.

family
pamilya

ham
hamon

aged Edam cheese
queso de bola

egg custard
leche flan

sweetened purple yam
halayang ube

The Muslims' Holiday Season

The Muslims of the Philippines celebrate Hari Raya Poasa, which ends the fasting period of Ramadan. Although it takes place in September, it is sort of like Christmas because it's a joyous time, and people celebrate with prayers and lots of food.

Also called *Eid al-Fitr*, people dress in their finest clothes for this festival. They adorn their homes with lights and decorations, give treats to children, and enjoy visits with friends and family.

dress for worship
abaya

sweet fried noodles
tinagtag

a sweet sticky-rice delicacy
dudol

traditional tribal tube skirt
malong

a skull cap
kufi

a head covering
hijab

a mosque
moske

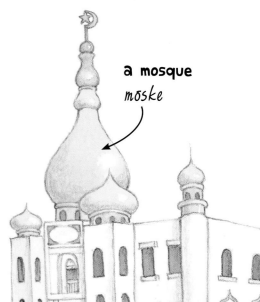

Happy New Year!
Manigong Bagong Taon!

On New Year's Eve Filipino families gather for a *medianoche* feast, usually with cousins, aunts and uncles, grandparents, and close friends. Together everyone practices a variety of traditions (or superstitions) intended to usher in a lucky new year. This is important because if we start off the new year badly, we will have bad luck for the rest of the year! A good number of these traditions are practiced by the Chinese during the Chinese New Year, which highlights the idea that Philippine culture is heavily influenced by Chinese culture.

fireworks
mga pailaw

jumping
pagtalon

Jumping up and down at the stroke of midnight will make you grow taller. The higher you jump, the taller you'll grow. Even the smallest children are pulled out of bed so that they, too, can jump and grow taller.

Why do people make loud noises on New Year's Eve?

Making loud noises by blowing a *torotot*, banging pots and pans, and lighting up *paputok* drives away bad spirits and bad luck.

firecrackers
mga paputok

a trumpet
torotot

pot lids
mga takip ng kaldero

42

uncle
tito

big brother
kuya

aunt
tita

father
tatay

mother
nanay

grandmother
lola

big sister
ate

relative
kamag-anak

round fruits
mga prutas na bilog
For good luck, display twelve different kinds of round fruits, each representing a month of the year.

wine
alak

New Year's Eve dinner
medianoche
a Spanish word referring to the midnight meal on New Year's Eve

fresh-coconut salad
buko salad

holiday beef roll
morcon

How to bring in good luck

a window
bintana

open
bukás

Shake coins while walking around the house.

Wear clothes with dots and other circular designs.

money
pera

a pocket
bulsa

Make sure your pocket and wallet are filled with money.

Scatter coins around the house.

coins
mga barya

Why do people open windows and doors on the first day of the new year?

Opening all the windows and doors to your house lets good luck flow in for the whole year.

For general good luck, eat twelve grapes at midnight.

grapes
ubas

a broom
walis tambo

Every Filipino house must be thoroughly cleaned before the first day of the year.

dragon dances
mga sayaw ng dragon
Dragon dances are performed in Manila's Chinatown to bring in good fortune for the new year.

The Chinese New Year

Chinese New Year, or Spring Festival, begins on the first day of the first month in the Chinese calendar and ends with the Lantern Festival fifteen days later. As in other countries with Chinese communities, Filipino-Chinese will spend a lot of money to decorate and buy presents, and—most important—to feast heartily. On the eve of the New Year families typically gather for a special dinner that almost always includes fish, dumplings, and lucky *tikoy*. Wishes for happiness, wealth, and longevity abound.

gift money
ang pao
good-luck money in red packets

sticky rice cake
tikoy
sticky rice cake, or *nián gāo*

Glossary

 **suman** sticky rice delicacy
Steamed sticky rice that comes in many forms but is always wrapped in leaves, oftentimes from the banana tree, before cooking.

 **magsasaka** a farmer

 **palayok** a clay pot
A traditional pot that is used for cooking food directly over a fire, as a serving dish at the table, or even as a *piñata* at children's parties.

 **kalabaw** a carabao or water buffalo
A farm animal used for pulling a plow through watery rice fields, and for hauling goods to the market.

 **ama or tatay** father or dad
In English there are many ways to address one's father: *dad*, *father*, *papa*, or even *pop*. In Filipino *tatay* is the less formal word.

 **kabayo** a horse

 **kawali** a frying pan
Any sort of pan used to cook over a fire or stove. It can be big or small, shallow or deep. A wok is one kind of *kawali*.

 **lechon** roast pig
All good *fiestas* feature a *lechon*—not only in the Philippines but also in Spain, Cuba, Puerto Rico, the Dominican Republic, and other Spanish-speaking nations.

higante a giant
The word *higante* describes someone with extremely large proportions; however, at this Philippine festival it refers to very tall painted figures made from bamboo, paper, resin, and clothing materials.

mga kandila candles
As in other cultures, candles are often used in religious ceremonies.

karera a race
Races are as popular in the Philippines as they are anywhere else in the world, whether they are car races, horse races, or triathlons.

mga singsing wedding rings

watawat a flag
Other words that mean flag are *bandila* and the Spanish word *bandera*.

pamasko Christmas present
Filipinos take gift-giving at Christmas so seriously that we have this word to specifically describe a present given for Christmas. A regular present is a *regalo*.

bata a child

salabat ginger tea
A hot beverage made from fresh ginger root.

mga bulaklak flowers

pamilya family
The Filipino family includes uncles, aunts, grandparents, cousins, and so on.

Published by Tuttle Publishing, an imprint of Periplus Editions (HK) Ltd.

www.tuttlepublishing.com

Library of Congress Cataloging-in-Publication Data

Romulo, Liana.
  Filipino celebrations / text by Liana Romulo ; illustrations by Corazon Dandan-Albano.
     48 p. : col. ill. ; 23 x 28 cm.
  ISBN 978-0-8048-3821-4 (hardcover)
1. Festivals--Philippines--Juvenile literature.
2. Philippines--Social life and customs--Juvenile literature. [1. Festivals--Philippines. 2. Holidays--Philippines. 3. Philippines--Social life and customs.] I. Dandan-Albano, Corazon, 1964- II. Title.
  GT4881.A2R66 2011
  394.269599--dc23

2011024139

ISBN: 978-0-8048-3821-4

Distributed by

North America, Latin America & Europe
Tuttle Publishing
364 Innovation Drive
North Clarendon, VT 05759-9436 U.S.A.
Tel: 1 (802) 773-8930;
Fax: 1 (802) 773-6993
info@tuttlepublishing.com
www.tuttlepublishing.com

Asia Pacific
Berkeley Books Pte. Ltd.
3 Kallang Sector #04-01
Singapore 349278
Tel: (65) 6741 2178
Fax: (65) 6741 2179
inquiries@periplus.com.sg
www.tuttlepublishing.com

24 23 22 21   2105TO
9 8 7 6 5

Printed in Malaysia

TUTTLE PUBLISHING® is a registered trademark of Tuttle Publishing, a division of Periplus Editions (HK) Ltd.

For Nimai and Sara.
With love.
C.D.A.